Customized Learning

Potential Air Force Applications

Thomas Manacapilli, Edward O'Connell,
Cheryl Benard

Prepared for the United States Air Force

Approved for public release; distribution unlimited

PROJECT AIR FORCE

The research described in this report was sponsored by the United States Air Force under Contract FA7014-06-C-0001. Further information may be obtained from the Strategic Planning Division, Directorate of Plans, Hq USAF.

Library of Congress Cataloging-in-Publication Data

Manacapilli, Thomas.
 Customized learning : potential Air Force applications / Thomas Manacapilli, Edward O'Connell, Cheryl Benard.
  p. cm.
 Includes bibliographical references and index.
 ISBN 978-0-8330-5061-8 (pbk. : alk. paper)
  . United States. Air Force--Airmen—Training of—Evaluation. 2. United States. Air Force. Air Education and Training Command--Evaluation. 3. Aeronautics, Military—Study and teaching—United States—Evaluation. I. O'Connell, Edward. II. Benard, Cheryl, 1953- III. Title..

 UG638.M318 2011
 358.4'150973—dc22

                                                                                           2010046000

Published 2011 by the RAND Corporation
1776 Main Street, P.O. Box 2138, Santa Monica, CA 90407-2138
1200 South Hayes Street, Arlington, VA 22202-5050
4570 Fifth Avenue, Suite 600, Pittsburgh, PA 15213-2665
RAND URL: http://www.rand.org/
To order RAND documents or to obtain additional information, contact
Distribution Services: Telephone: (310) 451-7002;
Fax: (310) 451-6915; Email: order@rand.org

Preface

The U.S. Air Force is arguably the best-trained air force in the world. But this comes at a price—initial skills training (IST) costs approximately $750 million per year. The Air Force has a continuing interest in reducing training costs while maintaining or improving the training product. This study looks at educational approaches that would customize training to the individual with the intent of minimizing the trainee's time in training, focusing the training on the trainee's needs, and getting the trainee productive sooner, all leading to reduced costs.

The research underlying this report was sponsored by the Directorate of Plans, Programs, and Analysis for Air Education and Training Command (AETC/A5/8/9). The research was conducted within the Manpower, Personnel, and Training Program of RAND Project AIR FORCE for the fiscal year 2009 study "Customized Learning for Airmen." This report should be of interest to Air Force leaders and staffs concerned with improving education and training.

RAND Project AIR FORCE

RAND Project AIR FORCE (PAF), a division of the RAND Corporation, is the U.S. Air Force's federally funded research and development center for studies and analyses. PAF provides the Air Force with independent analyses of policy alternatives affecting the development, employment, combat readiness, and support of current and future aerospace forces. Research is conducted in four programs: Force Modernization and Employment; Manpower, Personnel, and Training; Resource Management; and Strategy and Doctrine.

Additional information about PAF is available on our website:
http://www.rand.org/paf/

Contents

Figures

Tables

Summary

Background

In January 2008, Air Education and Training Command (AETC) published a white paper entitled "On Learning: The Future of Air Force Education and Training." Under its concept of *precision learning*, AETC envisions that

> Learning is customized to learner needs and abilities and delivered across a spectrum of live, virtual and constructive means using a variety of multi-media tools and modes. Learning is tailored to learners . . . by leveraging technology to deliver knowledge when, where and how needed. (pp. 13–14)

Around the same time, the National Academy of Engineering identified personal learning as one of 14 major challenges of the 21st century. And in February 2009, AETC/A5/8/9 asked RAND to look at the concept of *customized learning* (the Air Force's term for personalized learning) for application to Air Force training.

Motivation

The Air Force spends approximately $750 million per year on IST, plus an unknown amount for on-the-job and other types of training. This training has arguably helped make the U.S. Air Force the best air force in the world. However, current training methods may not be as efficient and effective as emerging alternatives. This study looks at educational approaches that would customize training to individual characteristics with the intent of minimizing the trainee's time in training, focusing the training on the trainee's needs, and getting the trainee productive sooner, all leading to reduced costs.

Context

The Air Force brings in approximately 34,000 new recruits each year. An individual is recruited and sent to a processing center where a job or job category is tentatively selected. The Air Force next sends the recruit, depending on a number of availability factors, to basic military training (BMT). During BMT, the career field is finalized, and on graduation (after approximately eight and one-half weeks), the student proceeds to the schoolhouse for job-specific training, also called IST.

IST can last as long as two years or as little as six weeks, depending on the specialty. All students in a particular course receive exactly the same training over exactly the same time.

The Air Force has an active program of on-the-job training and in-residence schools for special training. The Air Force also teaches professional military education to officer and enlisted personnel according to grade.

Analytic Approach

We approached the problem from three avenues:

1.   We talked to experts in and out of the military.
2.   We reviewed literature on personalized learning.
3.   We reviewed meta-analyses on case studies of personalized learning and assessed some contemporary models.

Understanding Customized Learning

The concept of personalized learning has a long history. There are two camps in the education community regarding this subject: the progressive movement dating back to John Dewey (which includes personalized learning concepts) and the uniform approach (skill and drill).

Some research suggests that, in the absence of severe mental retardation, students tend to learn in the same way but that everyone brings different predispositions and prior experience to the learning situation. So, learning is not based only on common cognitive ability but is also shaped by prior experience, unique skills, and individual talents. This leads to arguments for more-personalized learning pedagogies allowing students to progress at their own pace, given their prior experience, skills, and talents.

Other research suggests that students have learning styles that allow them to learn better when the environment and teaching styles match their learning styles. Additionally, many educators believe that there is a difference in how the millennial generation thinks, learns, and processes information. There is no direct evidence to support this claim as of yet, only an intuitive feel that this technology-savvy generation is different.

In 2004, Coffield et al., of the Learning and Skills Research Centre (LSRC), a UK-based organization, published an exhaustive report examining 71 learning styles from 2,800 references; the majority of studies were based on American research. The study categorized the 71 learning style theories into five families and then examined 13 styles across the five families in depth. Each learning style is associated with a theory of use and an instrument for testing the student to determine what style within the theory the student possesses. Table S.1 summarizes the results of their study.

Only one of the learning styles satisfied all of the criteria identified as important for proving the value of learning styles. This style, Allinson and Hayes, is more properly a tool for classification or selection of management personnel than a true learning style. Four of the styles met the study's criteria for predictive validity—individual scores were correlated with success in learning. Two of those styles belong to the family of constitutionally based learning styles—they are based on attributes that individuals are born with and do not change. In both

Table S.1
Evaluation of Representative Learning Style Theories

Theory/Instrument	Family	Internal Consistency	Test-Retest Reliability	Construct Validity	Predictive Validity
Allinson and Hayes	Flexibly stable	Yes	Yes	Yes	Yes
Apter	Stable personality	Yes	Yes	—	Yes
Dunn and Dunn	Constitutionally based	No	No	No	Yes
Entwistle	Learning approaches	Yes	—	Yes	No
Gregorc	Constitutionally based	No	No	No	Yes
Herrmann	Flexibly stable	—	Yes	Yes	—
Honey and Mumford	Flexibly stable	No	Yes	No	No
Jackson	Stable personality	—	—	—	—
Kolb	Flexibly stable	—	Yes	No	No
Myers-Briggs	Stable personality	Yes	Yes	No	No
Riding	Cognitive structures	No	No	No	No
Sternberg	Learning approaches	No	No	No	No
Vermunt	Learning approaches	Yes	Yes	Yes	No

SOURCE: Coffield et al., 2004a.

NOTE: Yes = criterion met; No = criterion not met; — = no evidence either way or issue still to be settled.

of the cases, though, the learning styles failed to meet the criteria of construct validity, which measures how well test scores can be interpreted as measuring what they intend to measure.

Conclusions

Our literature review leads us to conclude that attention to learning styles has potential benefit for the Air Force, but with limitations, and that the effectiveness of individualized teaching is often greatly exaggerated. We recommend that the Air Force conduct some experiments with Air Force vocational training before implementation across Air Force training is considered.

The use of learning style instruments does have positive impacts (self-awareness and meta-cognition), even when the case cannot be made as to why they would have impact.

Learning style feedback shows the student how to enhance his or her own learning, and it fosters a discourse between student and teacher on how the student can improve in a course.

Customized learning increases the probability of creating lifelong learners. As individuals discover their learning styles, they are motivated to use that knowledge. If they have had bad experiences in the past, the new knowledge gives them a fresh point at which to reengage in learning.

Attention to learning styles can be a catalyst for organizational and systemic change. New and better pedagogies have not been an active pursuit or subject of study for the Air Force. The Air Force needs an educational center of excellence for the study of new approaches to education and training. During the course of this study, the Air Force stood up an office in AETC for this purpose.

Learning styles can also provide a lexicon for dialogue between professional educators.

Implications

While the Air Force uses professional educators in some roles, it typically does not employ professional educators as instructors, but rather uses subject-matter experts to teach courses in initial skills and professional military education. Consequently, the majority of instructors do not have the expertise or ability to adapt their teaching style to a learning style.

The Air Force can take steps to lessen these concerns. First, the Air Force could update the Basic Instructor Course (BIC) with specific instruction on adapting teaching style to the style of the learners. Second, the Air Force could add additional instructor continuing education courses for the entire length of an instructor's tour. Third, the Air Force could hire educational mentors whose job would entail sitting in during instruction and constructively critiquing instructors on teaching effectiveness.

The Air Force operates a very structured IST process that requires each class of students to start and end courses together. The same is true for professional military education. The Air Force can run self-paced courses, as it did for some courses in the 1970s for initial skills training. We recommend that the Air Force perform an experiment on a self-paced initial skills course.

The eight-hour instructional day is too restrictive and does not give course managers or instructors the freedom to determine the best method or use of time to help students learn.

Customized learning does not have to be dependent on the instructor. Technology offers solutions that have not existed in the past. Technological solutions—software that adapts to the learner—can minimize the role of the instructor, thereby alleviating the need for professional educators. With appropriate technology, the instructor can take on the role of a coach or mentor with expertise in the subject area but without the need for unique teaching skills.

Customized Learning Applied to Air Force 2.0

Developing a learner-centric philosophy is a key component of customized learning. It shifts the relative importance from the process of transmitting information to the student to ensuring that the information is transmitted in a way that is best processed by the learner. It will require the new learning organization to create alternate means of conveying information such that the student can process information most effectively.

Customized learning will create new demands for an expanded knowledge base. Without argument, knowledge databases are critical to learning now and will be increasingly so in the future. One solution is to take advantage of the millennial generation's technological literacy and use it to create the knowledge databases of the future. Today's average instructor is becoming increasingly technologically literate and, perhaps, could develop computer-based instruction (CBI) and virtual world applications. Also, the software for CBI and virtual world development is increasingly user friendly. The Air Force needs to take advantage of software advances and a technologically literate force to develop the knowledge base of the future.

Customized learning could increase the need for knowledge-on-demand systems. It may be possible to move additional portions of IST into on-the-job training if knowledge systems are available for the Airmen to tap. With this approach, in addition to learning at their own pace and style, Airmen might also learn at a more propitious time.

Customized learning can improve education in the affective domain by making the learner the focus of the training and by giving the learner more control over the education process. As the organization communicates value to the individual, the individual is more likely to reciprocate and internalize the values of the organization.

The use of simulations can have a tremendous payoff. They provide an approach to learning that contrasts with the sterile environment of a lecture. They also provide users with a sense of the environment they will encounter on the job. Simulations can challenge users with virtual problem solving and virtual games, thereby increasing interest in the field of study.

The literature suggests that customized learning approaches motivate students to be continuous learners. Already today, young Airmen know how to find knowledge through the Internet. Most apply that ability to social networks and personal interests. It is a small step to apply that ability to job tasks, especially among motivated learners.

Technology Is Key

This report describes a number of tools and systems illustrative of emerging technological opportunities. For the Air Force, three insights are important: that new learning technologies hold the promise of mitigating some of the challenges its training programs confront by allowing greater responsiveness to the individual's learning style, prior knowledge, speed of learning, capabilities, and interests; that a very large pool of applications is available to draw upon and that these can also be adapted, or entirely new applications could be developed; but also that these applications are tools, not complete solutions. Overreliance on new learning technologies would not be a good idea.

Recommendations

We recommend that the Air Force take advantage of the new Advanced Learning Technology Demonstrations that AETC has established to test these ideas before large-scale implementation. There is much hyperbole regarding technology and new pedagogies. The best way to separate reality from hyperbole is to test the ideas in a real-world environment.

Acknowledgments

The idea and impetus for this study was provided by Maj Gen Erwin Lessel III, AETC/A5/8/9, Director of Plans, Programs, and Analysis for Air Education and Training Command. Members of his staff in AETC's Future Learning Division—Col John Thompson, Col Glenn Hover, and Wendy Johnson—were instrumental in providing direction and contacts for the research.

Jill Lindsey, Wright State University, helped form much of our initial thought and direction.

Andrew Fairbanks, IBM; Judy Brown, Army Distributed Learning Sub-Committee; Sumi Rush, Hi-Tech High School; Allison Rossett, San Diego State University; Paul Foster, University of Cincinnati; Jeanne Holm, NASA Jet Propulsion Laboratory; and Frank Moretti, Columbia University, were gracious to provide time to speak to us about the future of educational technologies.

Frank Coffield answered questions regarding his landmark work on learning styles for the Learning and Skills Research Centre in the UK.

Dietrich Albert, Cord Hockemeyer, and Stefanie Lindstaedt, Know-Center, Graz University of Technology, briefed us on technology initiatives by the Ministry of Education for the European Union.

Betty Hardman provided documentation describing the Air Force Basic Instructor Course.

Lt Col David Denhard, Peter Joffe, and other members of the AETC Studies and Analysis Squadron engaged us with tough questions and useful insights about the training process.

Finally, our fellow RAND researchers, Susan Bodilly, Michael Shanley, Lionel Galway, and Paul Howe, all assisted in a variety of ways.

Abbreviations

AETC	Air Education and Training Command
AETC/A5/8/9	Directorate of Plans, Programs, and Analysis for Air Education and Training Command
AETC/A8Q	Future Learning Division
AFSC	Air Force Specialty Code
AGE	Aerospace Ground Equipment course
ALTD	Advanced Learning Technology Demonstrations
BIC	Basic Instructor Course
BMT	basic military training
CBI	computer-based instruction
DfES	Department for Education and Skills [United Kingdom]
DLI	Defense Language Institute
IST	initial skills training
JPL	Jet Propulsion Laboratory
LMS	learning management system
LSA	Learning Style Analysis [Prashnig trademark]
LSRC	Learning and Skills Research Centre
NAE	National Academy of Engineering
NASA	National Aeronautics and Space Administration
PAF	Project AIR FORCE
SRPL	self-regulated personalized learning
VAKT	visual, auditory, kinesthetic, and tactile

CHAPTER ONE

Introduction

Background

In January 2008, Air Education and Training Command (AETC) published a white paper entitled "On Learning: The Future of Air Force Education and Training." The paper presented three concepts and a number of new approaches for the future of education and training in the Air Force. Under its concept of *precision learning*, AETC envisioned "learning tailored to the learner needs and abilities and delivered across a spectrum of live, virtual, and constructive means." The white paper emphasizes AETC's desire to leapfrog learning using a combination of technology and new pedagogical concepts.

In 2008, the National Academy of Engineering (NAE) identified personal learning as one of 14 major challenges of the 21st century. In a similar vein, in February 2009, the Directorate of Plans, Programs, and Analysis for Air Education and Training Command (AETC/A5/8/9) asked RAND to look at the concept of customized learning for application to Air Force Training.[1] We were asked to provide a definition of customized learning in an Air Force context (with a focus on learning styles), an assessment of its potential utility to the Air Force, a list of hindrances to Air Force use of customized learning, and suggestions for a way forward.

Motivation

The Air Force spends approximately $750 million a year on initial skills training (IST), plus an unknown amount for on-the-job and other types of training. This training has arguably helped make the U.S. Air Force the best air force in the world. However, current training methods may not be as efficient and effective as emerging alternatives. This study looks at educational approaches that would customize training to individual characteristics with the intent of minimizing the trainee's time in training, focusing the training on the trainee's needs, and getting the trainee productive sooner, all leading to reduced costs.

There are anecdotal claims that the "millennial generation" thinks differently, and that new approaches are needed to maintain the interest and attention of its members. Customized learning that capitalizes on new technologies may work better for millennial learners.

---

[1] The Air Force uses the term *customized learning* instead of *personalized learning*. It has the same general definition. It is tailoring the instruction to the individual in a manner that allows the student to learn in his or her most optimal manner.

Context

The Air Force brings in approximately 34,000 new recruits each year. An individual is recruited and sent to a processing center where a job or job category is tentatively selected. The Air Force next sends the recruit to basic military training (BMT). During BMT, the career field is finalized, and on graduation (after approximately eight and one-half weeks), the student proceeds to the schoolhouse for job-specific training, also called IST.

IST can last as long as two years or as little as six weeks, depending on the specialty. All students in a course receive exactly the same training over exactly the same time. Most instruction is delivered by PowerPoint lecture. There is also hands-on instruction to reinforce lectures.

The majority of instructors are not professional educators. Most are military members who instruct for three to four years before returning to field duties. To prepare them for their role as instructors, they attend a one-month Basic Instructor Course (BIC). They also usually audit the class they are going to teach, prior to actually instructing.

The Air Force has an active program of on-the-job training and in-residence schools for special training. Nearly 150,000 students are involved in distance learning or in-residence training each year.

The Air Force also teaches professional military education to more than 20,000 personnel each year. There are separate schools for officer and enlisted personnel according to grade.

Analytic Approach

We approached our task from three avenues:

1. We talked to experts in and out of the military.
2. We reviewed literature on personalized learning.
3. We reviewed meta-analyses on cases studies of personalized learning and assessed some contemporary models.

Expert Visits
We first visited a dozen experts in the field to get their thoughts on personalized learning and the potential impact of technology on learning. We used those ideas to direct further research.

Literature Review
We next reviewed more than 300 documents regarding learning style or customized learning. During the course of our research, we discovered several meta-analyses of learning styles, some of them fairly recent and of good utility. One of the best was Coffield et al. (2004a), which identified 71 models of learning styles and categorized them into five categories or "families." It then focused on 13 of the learning styles, representative of the five families.[2]

---

[2]   One possible concern might be that we relied too much on European studies, especially Coffield et al.'s research, which was conducted at the UK-based Learning and Skills Research Centre (LSRC), and that the results might reflect European applications and not American. According to one of the authors we contacted, Frank Coffield, the LSRC study is actually based on a "clear majority of [American] cases rather than British or Australian [material]."

Organization of This Report

In Chapter Two of this report we look at the history of customized learning and recent meta-analyses of its effectiveness. In Chapter Three we discuss the implications of implementing customized learning in the current Air Force education and training process. In Chapter Four we examine our conclusions regarding the effectiveness of customized learning in the context of the new Air Force 2.0 concept. In Chapter Five we discuss technological solutions for improving Air Force education and training based on the conclusions we have drawn in this study. Chapter Six provides specific recommendations for educational experiments.

CHAPTER TWO

Understanding Customized Learning

Background

The concept of personalized learning has a long history. There are two basic camps in the education community regarding this subject: the progressive movement dating back to John Dewey (which includes personalized learning concepts) and the uniform approach ("skill and drill"). The perspective we have adopted, widely supported in the current literature, is that personalized learning is more effective than skill and drill.

The science suggests that, in the absence of severe mental retardation, students tend to learn in the same way but that everyone brings different predispositions and prior experiences to the learning situation. Thus, learning is not based only on common cognitive ability but is also shaped by prior experience, unique skills, and individual talents. Given this, in any heterogeneous grouping of students, some will have significant prior experience with the subject to be learned or will have the background and inclinations to grasp the concepts quickly. Others will struggle to pick up the basic concepts and will lag behind. Some students learn specific material at a much faster rate than others. Some will pick up a subject quickly while others struggle. Some will gain mastery in one field while others gain mastery in another. This leads to arguments for more-personalized learning pedagogies allowing students to progress at their own pace, given their prior experience, skills, and talents. This does not imply that the bar for passing or the standard for mastery should change but that the speed at which each student progresses and the amount of effort required can vary.

Technology-supported learning advances these concepts by using media (television, computers, distance learning) to present a curriculum module to multiple individuals within their own control, allowing them to self-pace.[1] More-sophisticated versions, usually computer based, allow immediate feedback; additional tutorials for extra practice or to explain concepts with which the student is struggling; ongoing assessment; and significantly reduced operating cost per student, exclusive of the costs of development and equipment. (This assumes that a supervisor is not needed for adult students who are well motivated and self-disciplined, thus reducing labor costs.) Furthermore, technology facilitates a customized curriculum where the student, with advice and approval, can avoid repetition of what he or she already knows and can instead pick and choose among topics that will most further his or her career or learning objectives.[2]

---

[1] Technology-supported learning is complementary to personalized learning. Intelligent tutoring systems allow the tailoring of instruction to the student that has not been possible in the past.

[2] Pretesting is primarily applicable to skills-based training. In some cases of complex training, such as leader development, it may not be advisable.

To a significant extent, this technology-supported learning is already used in the Air Force[3] and in many schools in such applications as computer-based tutorials or instruction with variations in speed, material presented depending on responses, and immediate feedback from computerized testing. In the civilian sector, the University of Phoenix now has the largest enrollment in the country and uses many aspects of personal pacing and customized curriculum packaging. The Air Force and other branches of the military use distance learning for some courses.

Recognized Importance

The U.S. Department of Education recognizes the importance of taking advantage of customized learning approaches in education systems. It sees technology as the key to customizing learning.

> Harnessing the power of innovation for the good of our schools is not just a novel enterprise. The nation's health and prosperity depend on it. By leveraging technology, schools can customize instruction and ensure that children who need extra help get it. (U.S. Department of Education, 2008, p. 1)

The NAE named personalized learning as one of the 14 great challenges of the 21st century. It also recognizes the potential of technology to match content to the learner.

> In recent years, a growing appreciation of individual preferences and aptitudes has led toward more "personalized learning," in which instruction is tailored to a student's individual needs. Personal learning approaches range from modules that students can master at their own pace to computer programs designed to match the way it presents content with a learner's personality. (National Academy of Engineering of the National Academies, 2009)

But while we are seeing advances of technology in the classroom, experts do not yet see the full payoff expected from that investment.

> Education is not a one-size-fits-all enterprise. Just as every child has unique needs, so does every teacher, every school, every district and every state. While real progress has been made in wiring our classrooms and equipping them with new technologies, *we have yet to see a profound transformation in the way we deliver education.* (U.S. Department of Education, 2008, p. 1, emphasis ours)

The potential of customized learning is that, combined with technology, it can perhaps help to indeed realize a transformation in education.

Defining Customized Learning

In developing a definition for customized learning, we searched the literature for those most widely used. Below is a sampling of some of these definitions.

---

[3] The Air Force invests in distance learning through satellite broadcasts and computer-based instruction (CBI).

Personalized learning occurs when . . . students assess themselves and their community in order to design learning opportunities that fit their own aspirations, talents, and interests—while they also gather evidence to show that they are meeting academic expectations. (Clark, 2003, p. 12)

Taking a highly structured and responsive approach to each child's and young person's learning, in order that all are able to progress, achieve and participate. It means strengthening the link between learning and teaching by engaging pupils—and their parents—as partners in learning. (Gilbert, 2006, p. 6)

According to the United Kingdom's Department for Education and Skills (DfES), there are five key components of personalized learning, which need to be embedded in whole school policy and practice to enhance learning outcomes:

1. Assessment for learning: teachers and learners identifying areas of strength and learning needs, and setting targets. . . .
2. Effective teaching and learning strategies: developing a repertoire of skills to actively engage and stretch learners, building on their prior knowledge and experience, and incorporating individual and group activity. . . .
3. Curriculum entitlement and choice: personal and flexible learning pathways through the education system. . . .
4. School organization: models which empower pupils, supporting high quality teaching and learning, and pupil welfare. . . .
5. Strong partnership beyond the school . . . . (Field, 2006)

The DfES defines personalized learning as being

about tailoring education to individual need, interest and aptitude so as to ensure that every pupil achieves and reaches the highest standards possible, notwithstanding their background or circumstances, and right across the spectrum of achievement. (Space for Personalised Learning, 2007, p. 13)

Personalized Learning is a unique, blended classroom-based and non-classroom-based public educational model that is tailored to the needs and interests of each individual student. Personalized Learning is a 21st century, "on the leading edge" approach to public education that honors and recognizes the unique gifts, skills, passions, and attributes of each child. Personalized Learning is dedicated to developing individualized learning programs for each child whose intent is to engage each child in the learning process in the most productive and meaningful way to optimize each child's learning potential and success. (Association of Personalized Learning Services, 2009)

Nearly all of these definitions put the priority on the learner. The learner and the learner's success as an individual are the focus, and everything is tailored for and to the learner. The learner is an active partner in the process and not a passive recipient. In light of these definitions and others in the literature, we propose that a definition of *customized learning* for the Air Force include the following elements:

- making Airmen aware of their optimal learning styles, helping them understand how they learn best, and involving them actively in the learning process with the goal of developing lifelong, continuous learners
- making instructors aware of their teaching styles, using varying modes of instruction (different speeds, forms of knowledge transmission, and the delivery domain, i.e., institutional, operational, and self-development) geared to varying subject matter, Airmen learning needs, and Airmen learning styles.

Effectively executed, it should personally connect students to what they are learning so that they are motivated and challenged to learn.

Research on Learning Styles

A key element of customized learning is its focus on individuals' varying *learning styles*, i.e., their approaches to absorbing learning. In an extensive meta-analysis of this research, Coffield et al. (2004a) argued that if educators understand how students learn best, they can adapt teaching styles to learner styles to maximize the information intake of the learners. Coffield et al. identified 71 models of learning styles and categorized them into five families. They then focused on a smaller subset, representative of the five families. Within the five families, they identified 13 representative models. Figure 2.1 presents the five families and the initial 71 models.

The first family of models presented in the left column of Figure 2.1 represents learning styles based on genetic and other constitutionally based factors. Essentially, these are factors and traits with which people are born.

The second family shares the view that learning styles are a product of the individual's cognitive structure. As with the first family of models, advocates of these models hold that a person's learning style is not easily changed.

The third family represents models that focus on the observable parts of a relatively stable personality type. One of the better known examples is the Myers-Brigg personality test.

In the fourth family, learning styles are not considered fixed traits. The individual's preference for learning is thought to change depending on the situation. For the most part, though, the styles are generally considered stable over long periods.

The fifth family focuses on approaches to or strategies for learning. Advocates of these models hold that previous experiences, the subject being studied, and culture determine effective teaching approaches.

Figure 2.1
Breakout of Learning Style Models

Learning styles and preferences are largely **constitutionally based,** including the four modalities: VAKT.	Learning styles reflect deep-seated features of the **cognitive structure,** including "patterns of ability."	Learning styles are one component of a relatively **stable personality type.**	Learning styles are **flexibly stable learning preferences.**	Move on from learning styles to **learning approaches, strategies, orientations,** and **conceptions of learning.**
Dunn and Dunn	**Riding**	**Apter**	**Allinson and Hayes**	**Entwistle**
Gregorc	Broverman	**Jackson**	**Herrmann**	**Sternberg**
Bartlett	Cooper	**Myers-Briggs**	**Honey and Mumford**	**Vermunt**
Betts	Gardner et al.	Epstein and Meier	**Kolb**	Biggs
Gordon	Guilford	Harrison-Branson	Felder and Silverman	Conti and Kolody
Marks	Holzman and Klein	Miller	Hermanussen, Wierstra, de Jong, and Thijssen	Grasha-Riechmann
Paivio	Hudson		Kaufmann	Hill
Richardson	Hunt		Kirton	Marton and Säljö
Sheehan	Kagan		McCarthy	McKenney and Keen
Torrance	Kogan			Pask
	Messick			Pintrich, Smith, Garcia, and McCeachie
	Pettigrew			Schmeck
	Witkin			Weinstein, Zimmerman, and Palmer
				Whetton and Cameron

SOURCE: Coffield et al., 2004a.
NOTES: VAKT = visual, auditory, kinesthetic, and tactile. Learning styles in bold are those that best represent each group.
RAND *TR880-2.1*

Measuring Effectiveness

In evaluating the effectiveness of learning style models, Coffield et al. evaluated 351 sources, the large majority being American educational studies, evaluating the learning style models on design, validity,[4] reliability,[5] implications of pedagogy, and evidence of pedagogy.

Evaluation Criteria

Each of the 13 models and their accompanying diagnostic instruments were then summarized on four measures:

---

[4]   There were three aspects of validity: construct validity, face validity, and predictive validity. In construct validity, the concern is whether the items on the learning style diagnostic instruments capture the important attributes of the learning styles in the applicable model. Face validity differs from construct validity in that face validity shows support for an assessment tool based on common-sense judgment that the items in the tool appear to measure what they claim to measure. Predictive validity is concerned with whether attention to varying learning styles produces the expected changes in task performance (Coffield et al., 2004a).

[5]   Reliability was another important concern of the study. Many learning style claims are extrapolated or generalized to other situations that were not tested. The study specifically considered whether results could be suitably extrapolated to other conditions—that is, can instructors apply their adaptation to learning styles in other contexts with similar results?

- Internal consistency, or internal reliability, is the degree to which the items in the diagnostic instrument measure the same thing. This is measured by the average correlation between each item and all the other items.
- Test-retest reliability measures the stability of the instrument scores as indicated by read-ministering the instrument to the same group and calculating the correlation coefficient using the two sets of scores.
- Construct validity evaluates how far scores on an instrument can be interpreted as measuring only what they are intended to measure. Cross-correlations, with known variables that are related, are used to determine this measure.
- Predictive validity measures the extent to which scores on an instrument or application of a model would predict learning outcomes.

A large number of injunctions and claims for pedagogy emerge from the research . . . , although many theorists draw logical conclusions about practice from their models of learning styles, there is a dearth of well-conducted experimental studies of alternative approaches derived from particular models. Moreover, most of the empirical studies have been conducted on university students in departments of psychology or business studies; and some would criticize these as studies of captive and perhaps atypical subjects presented with contrived tasks. (Coffield et al., 2004a, p. 4)

Table 2.1 is a summary of the results of the study for the 13 models. Individual studies on each model were evaluated and assigned one of three scores: met criteria, failed to meet criteria, or the evidence was insufficient to make a conclusion. The report contains additional evaluative information on each of the learning style models.

The learning style models failed to meet all four criteria, with the exception of Allinson and Hayes. The premise of their model is that the balance between intuition and analysis used by individuals in their thinking and decisionmaking is the most fundamental dimension of cognitive style. Their 38-item instrument allows three responses (true, uncertain, and false) to statements that characterize an individual's cognitive styles. Table 2.2 lists some of their items.

The Allinson and Hayes model categorizes individuals into right-brained, intuition-based individuals or left-brained, analysis-based individuals. While there is very strong evidence supporting the Allinson and Hayes model, the problem with its use in an Air Force context is that it is more applicable to management and job selection than to pedagogy.

Apter's model met the criteria for three measures, with incomplete evidence regarding construct validity, but Apter's "Reversal theory" is a theory of personality, not of learning style. A key premise is that learning cannot be understood in isolation from motivation. Apter's theory utilizes four domains with eight associated needs and corresponding styles at each end of the domain. An additional six styles complete the theory (Figure 2.2).

In Figure 2.2, the first four groupings are eight styles based in four experiential domains (Coffield et al., 2004b). Style groupings five and six are polar opposite styles. The latter set of groupings represent tendencies rather than psychological needs but are also called styles. In total, Apter's Motivational Style Profile measures 14 styles and further adds derived measures, among which are key educational components, such as achievement, motivation, boredom, frustration, and satiation. Coffield et al. concluded that the implications have not been fully elaborated or widely researched. A possible implication for the Air Force could be in classification, especially as it relates to long courses where motivation is a key component of success.

Table 2.1
Evaluation of Representative Learning Style Models

Theory/Instrument	Family	Internal Consistency	Test-Retest Reliability	Construct Validity	Predictive Validity
Allinson and Hayes	Flexibly stable	Yes	Yes	Yes	Yes
Apter	Stable personality	Yes	Yes	—	Yes
Dunn and Dunn	Constitutionally based	No	No	No	Yes
Entwistle	Learning approaches	Yes	—	Yes	No
Gregorc	Constitutionally based	No	No	No	Yes
Herrmann	Flexibly stable	—	Yes	Yes	—
Honey and Mumford	Flexibly stable	No	Yes	No	No
Jackson	Stable personality	—	—	—	—
Kolb	Flexibly stable	—	Yes	No	No
Myers-Briggs	Stable personality	Yes	Yes	No	No
Riding	Cognitive structures	No	No	No	No
Sternberg	Learning approaches	No	No	No	No
Vermunt	Learning approaches	Yes	Yes	Yes	No

SOURCE: Coffield et al., 2004a.

NOTE: Yes = criterion met; No = criterion not met; — = no evidence either way or issue still to be settled. The evaluations were external in all cases, meaning that they explored the theory or instruments associated with a model but were not managed or supervised by the originator(s) of that model.

Table 2.2
Sample Statements from the Allinson and Hayes Cognitive Style Index

Cognitive Style	Statement
Analysis	I find detailed, methodological work satisfying.
	I am careful to follow rules and regulations at work.
	When making a decision, I take my time and thoroughly consider all relevant factors.
	My philosophy is that it is better to be safe than risk being sorry.
Intuition	I make decisions and get on with things rather than analyze every last detail.
	I find that "too much analysis results in paralysis."
	My "gut feeling" is just as good a basis for decisionmaking as careful analysis.
	I make many of my decisions on the basis of intuition.

SOURCE: Coffield et al., 2004a.

Figure 2.2
Apter's Reversal Theory of Motivational Styles

Need style	Achievement Serious	⟷	Fun Playful
Need style	Fitting in Conforming	⟷	Freedom Challenging
Need style	Power Competitive	⟷	Love Affectionate
Need style	Individuation Self-oriented	⟷	Transcendence Other-oriented
Style	Arousal-avoidance	⟷	Arousal-seeking
Style	Optimism	⟷	Pessimism
Style	Arousability	⟷	Effortfulness

RAND *TR880-2.2*

Two additional models showed predictive validity but failed in other measures. Both (Dunn and Dunn; Gregorc) are from the constitutionally based family.

The Dunn and Dunn model has four main elements: environmental, sociological, emotional, and physical modality preferences. The environmental element includes noise level, lighting, temperature, and classroom design features. The sociological element contains preferences toward groups, authority figures, routine or variety in learning, and motivational reasons (to please parents, teachers, or authority figures). The emotional element looks at academic motivation (need to achieve academic success), responsibility, persistence, and need for structure. The last element, physical modality preferences, includes ways to learn (auditory, visual, tactile, and kinesthetic), food intake (need to eat while concentrating), time of day, and mobility (need to move). Lovelace (2005) conducted a meta-analysis of the Dunn and Dunn model. Her research (p. 180) concluded that "the Dunn and Dunn Learning-Style Model is both a practically and educationally significant construct that improves student achievements and attitudes toward learning."

The Gregorc model also showed positive results in some studies. Drysdale, Ross, and Shulz (2001), in a study of first-year college students, found that the model could predict the performance in 11 of 19 subject areas. Gregorc identified four categories of learners: abstract sequential (logical, analytical, rational, and evaluative), abstract random (sensitive, colorful, emotional, and spontaneous), concrete sequential (ordered, perfection-oriented, practical, and thorough), and concrete random (intuitive, independent, impulsive, and original). Those individuals identified as concrete sequential did very well in scientific, technological, or mathematical subject areas. There are implications for the Air Force in the classification of concrete sequential learners into technologically difficult career fields.

Quality of the Research

Despite the large amount of information available, Coffield et al. (2004a) found the body of studies on learning styles to be lacking in robustness.

It is important to note that the field of learning styles research as a whole is characterized by a very large number of small-scale applications of particular models to small samples of students in specific contexts. This has proved especially problematic for our review of evidence of the impact of learning styles on teaching and learning, since there are very few robust studies which offer, for example, reliable and valid evidence and clear implications for practice based on empirical findings. (p. 1)

Clark (2008) argues that adjusting learning for learning styles does not systematically increase learning and that giving the learner control over the sequence of instruction or the content itself can actually harm instruction. But he also concedes that giving students control over the pace of learning helps maintain challenge.

Recognizing extensive disagreement in the literature regarding the claims of personalized learning, Coffield et al. (2004a) reached a candid assessment.

We have found the field to be much more extensive, opaque, contradictory and controversial than we thought at the start of the research process. Evaluating different models of learning styles and their implications for pedagogy requires an appreciation of this complexity and controversy. It also requires some understanding of ideas about learning and measurement that have preoccupied researchers in education, psychology and neuroscience for decades. (p. 2)

The benefits of individualized teaching are often greatly exaggerated, although many teachers will admit that it is extremely difficult to ensure that learners are benefiting from specially tailored approaches when there is a large class to manage. (p. 133)

A Useful Model for the Air Force

One model not included in the Coffield et al. meta-analysis but that nonetheless caught our attention because of its comprehensiveness was Prashnig's Learning Style Analysis (LSA) Pyramid (Prashnig, undated). As depicted in Figure 2.3, this analysis assesses 49 individual elements in six areas. Four areas fall into the biologically or genetically determined area, and two areas are based on conditioned or learned behavior. In essence, her model cuts across two of the "families" evaluated by Coffield et al. Additionally, the constitutionally based models had predictive validity (see Table 2.1), meaning that student and instructor awareness of the learning style had positive effects on educational effectiveness.

The following description is adapted from Prashnig's Creative Learning Center website:

- The first area at the top of the chart is left/right brain dominance. LSA assesses sequential or simultaneous brain processing strategies, reflective or impulsive thinking styles, and overall analytic or holistic/global learning styles.
- The second area is sensory modalities, including auditory (hearing, talking, inner dialogue), visual (reading, seeing, visualizing), tactile (manipulating, touching), and kinesthetic (doing, feeling) preferences.
- The third area is physical needs, including identifying needs for mobility (preferences for moving around or remaining seated/stationary), intake (eating, nibbling, drinking, chewing, etc.), and time of day preferences (personal biorhythm).

Figure 2.3
Prashnig's Learning Style Analysis Pyramid

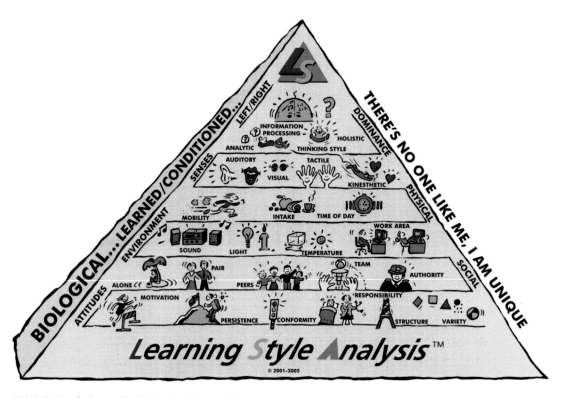

SOURCE: Prashnig, undated. Used with permission.
RAND *TR880-2.3*

- The fourth area is environment, relating to preferences for sound (needing music/sound/ ambient noise or wanting it quiet), light (needing bright or dim lighting), temperature (needing cool or warm), and work area (wanting formal or informal/comfortable design).
- The fifth area is social groupings, including preferences for working alone, in a pair, with peers, or in a team, and authority (wanting to learn with a teacher or parent, or autonomously).
- The last area represented in the diagram is attitudes, including motivation (internally or externally motivated for learning), persistence (high, fluctuating, or low), conformity (conforming or nonconforming/rebellious), structure (being self-directed or needing directions and guidance from others), and variety (needing routine or changes and variety).

Prashnig and her colleagues have created diagnostic instruments to determine an individual's learning profile on all of the categories shown. Such instruments can provide the learner with useful insights on how he or she learns best. Testing instruments can be used by instructors and can even be embedded in CBI.

Educational Intervention Effects and Customized Learning

In a meta-analysis of various educational interventions, Hattie (1999) found useful effects with a customized learning focus but also found a number of interventions with higher immediate payoffs. In Table 2.3, interventions are ranked by effect size.[6]

Four of these interventions embody aspects of customized learning:

- **Direct instruction.** Customized learning includes teaching material directly to the student in a style with which the student is most comfortable.
- **Student's disposition to learn.** It is possible that customized learning can increase the motivation of students to learn through greater understanding of themselves as learners.
- **Class environment.** A few of the learning styles suggest that some students learn better in different environments or at different times of day.
- **Teacher style.** Customized learning encourages the use of different teaching styles to match the student learning style.

While these four are useful, Hattie finds other strong effects for interventions that are not directly related to customized learning. The largest increase is for reinforcement efforts.

Table 2.3
Educational Intervention Effect

Intervention	Effect Size
Reinforcement	1.13
Student's prior cognitive ability	1.04
Instructional quality	1.00
Direct instruction	0.82
Student's disposition to learn	0.61
Class environment	0.56
Peer tutoring	0.50
Parental involvement	0.46
Teacher style	0.42
Affective attributes of students	0.24
Individualization	0.14
Behavioral objectives	0.12
Team teaching	0.06

SOURCE: Hattie, 1999.

---

[6]   Hattie interprets effect size as follows:

> An effect size of 1.0 indicates an increase of one standard deviation, typically associated with advancing children's achievement by one year, improving the rate of learning by 50%, or a correlation between some variable (e.g., amount of homework) and achievement of approximately .50. When implementing a new program, an effect size of 1.0 would mean that approximately 95% of outcomes positively enhance achievement, or average students receiving that treatment would exceed 84% of students not receiving that treatment. (1999, p. 4)

Instructional quality is the third highest intervention effect, and yet current practice in the Air Force gives instructors only one four-week course for the entire four-year instructor assignment. These varying intervention effects highlight the need for experimentation before settling on any intervention as a primary tool for improving education and training.

Conclusions

Our literature review leads us to conclude that attention to learning styles has potential benefit for the Air Force, but with limitations, and that the effectiveness of individualized teaching is often greatly exaggerated. While the range of studies focused on high school and above, we think some prudent experiments with Air Force technical training are necessary before implementation across Air Force training should be considered. AETC's Advanced Learning Technology Demonstrations (ALTD) program is the right place to test these proposals.[7]

The use of learning style instruments and the application of their underlying theories can have positive impacts. One can conjecture that providing information to the students on how they learn benefits the students by providing self-awareness and metacognition.[8] Learning style feedback shows students how to enhance their own learning, and it fosters a discourse between students and teachers on how to improve learning (Coffield et al., 2004a, p. 119). Additionally, customized learning increases the probability of creating lifelong learners. As individuals learn about their individual learning styles, they are motivated to use that knowledge for better learning (Coffield et al., 2004a, pp. 119, 132).

Coffield et al. argues that attention to learning styles can be a catalyst for organizational and systemic change (2004a, p. 133). A focus such as this could lead to new approaches to education and training in the Air Force. During the course of this study, AETC stood up its Future Learning Division (AETC/A8Q), staffed with educational experts, for this purpose. Additionally, the AETC Studies and Analysis Squadron can assist in developing experimental designs for testing education proposals and analyzing the results. Provided the costs of experimentation are low, attention to learning styles may still prove to have measureable impacts on graduation success.

Finally, learning styles provide a lexicon for dialogue among professional educators. Technology, new pedagogies, and improvements to classroom practices can be explored more effectively if the terms and elements are better defined and understood (Coffield et al., 2004a, p. 120).

---

7   AETC has recently started a program to test educational interventions and strategies in pilot programs.

8   Metacognition is the awareness and conscious use of the psychological processes involved in perception, memory, thinking, and learning (Coffield et al., 2004a).

CHAPTER THREE

Implications of Employing Customized Learning in the Air Force

Our literature review led us to recommend the application of customized learning in a limited sense. Because of limitations in the instructor force (discussed below), we recommend that the Air Force explore adapting teaching styles to learner styles using properly scoped pilot projects supported by experimentation in order to fill the current research gap in an Air Force context. If the Air Force decides to shift its training more toward customized learning, a number of implications arise. In this chapter, we discuss some of those implications for instructor qualifications and classroom practice.

Instructor Qualifications

The Air Force generally does not employ professional educators as technical training instructors. Each Air Force course utilizes individuals previously employed in their respective specialties to instruct new students. These instructors are assigned to a three- or four-year tour as a temporary, career-broadening opportunity. The instructor receives four weeks of training in a BIC and audits the class he or she will teach. Few have any background in education, and most have only an associate's degree. Consequently, the majority of instructors may not have the expertise to adapt their teaching style to a learner style, let alone to do so in a class of eight or more students.

While the structure of Air Force institutional instruction may not lend itself to implementing all available approaches to adapting teaching styles to learning styles, instructors can benefit from the awareness of their own teaching styles and gaps therein using readily available self-assessment tools. They can then implement many simple techniques to increase engagement with their students after taking into account the individual student learning style and group learning style profile. There are some civilian instructors, but they represent a small percentage of the total force, and most of these are also not professional educators (i.e., they do not hold a degree in education).

In contrast to AETC, the Defense Language Institute (DLI) uses career civilians as instructors, some of whom are professional educators. DLI employs customized learning quite extensively. Each of the students is tested for his or her learning style, and the instructors do adapt their teaching to the student. But DLI also has very small classes (one to six students).

There are some relatively simple, low-cost ways in which the Air Force could enable its technical instructors to perform better. First, the Air Force could update BIC by using LSA[1]

---

[1] For more information on LSA, see Figure 2.3.

assessments to inform instructors of their specific learning styles, possible gaps, and simple techniques to apply based on best practices. This would include instruction on how to adapt teaching styles to the style of learners and groups of learners. Second, the Air Force could add continuing education courses throughout their tenure as instructors, as opposed to the one four-week course used now. Third, the Air Force could hire (or designate) educational mentors whose job would entail sitting in on the courses and constructively supporting and mentoring the instructors on their teaching effectiveness. While training advisors are present in training squadrons, it is not clear that the personnel assigned to this duty are well grounded in education theory and practice. DLI uses department heads for a similar function, with a requirement of observing each instructor once a quarter.

Classroom Instruction

When applied to a technical training context, we found that customized learning has implications for class scheduling, the length of the training day, and the use of classroom technology.

Class Scheduling

One approach to customized learning, which even its detractors admit is effective (Clark, 2008), is self-paced learning. Unfortunately, the Air Force operates a very structured training process that requires each class of students to start and end courses together. An individual who could learn faster is not permitted to advance more rapidly, while an individual who learns more slowly also cannot work at the optimal pace, often resulting in being "washed back" to repeat the block of instruction.[2] In the mid-1970s, the enlisted personnel course was self-paced, but it does not appear that any initial skills courses today are self-paced, nor are the resident professional military education programs. We recommend that the Air Force experiment with a self-paced initial skills course.

The Air Force uses a self-paced, distance learning approach (the correspondence method) for most of its officer nonresident professional military education programs. It also uses self-pacing for Airmen in on-the-job training to upgrade from level 3, apprentice, to level 5, journeyman. None of the residence courses has any self-pacing within the course.

Allowing students to work at their own pace in a technical training course would result in some students finishing a course sooner and some later than normal but should not affect the overall rate of students reporting to their first duty station. Within some limitations, courses could start at any moment, alleviating some classification issues.[3] It would also make classification for those Air Force Specialty Codes (AFSCs) simpler, since hard class-start dates would not be a limiting factor. For training tracks containing multiple courses, this approach has the added benefit of allowing washbacks to immediately restart a course without having to wait for a fixed class start. The literature suggests that many students would graduate sooner. The Navy found reductions in time to train of 10 to 30 percent with no effect on success and found significant cost savings without decreasing the number of instructors (Carey et al., 2007).

---

[2]   Sitzmann (2006) found that web-based instruction and classroom instruction were equally effective, and in long courses where the trainee was provided control, web-based instruction was more effective.

[3]   One of the difficulties in training management is matching a person's qualifications to class openings to minimize waiting time after completion of basic military training.

Another approach is blended learning or hybrid courses, in which some of the material is taught via other methods prior to and after the students attend a brick-and-mortar school.

Eight-Hour Instructional Day

The eight-hour instructional day, as currently mandated for technical training, is inconsistent with a customized learning approach for two reasons. First, it does not give the instructors the freedom to customize the length of training to fit the course content. As an example, in the Air Traffic Control course, there are six hours of instruction followed by two hours of simulation to reinforce the instruction. In this course, the eight-hour instructional day makes sense. But in other courses, such as operations intelligence, the course is primarily focused on memorization. There is a limit to how much information can be memorized in a day. This course might have better results with a shorter instructional day that allowed the students time to meet with the instructor for specialized instruction or to internalize the information in a less structured format.

Second, the eight-hour training day tends to reduce student and instructor interface outside the classroom. Instructors interviewed in a separate RAND study remarked that the eight-hour training day allows very little time for personalized help. In the past, when the Air Force ran six-hour instructional days, time was available in an instructor's normal duty day to help students who were struggling. Though the term was not used, in a sense that extra time was dedicated to a kind of personalized learning.

Classroom Technology

Customized learning does not have to be dependent on the instructor. Technology offers some possibilities. For example, in 2004, the European Community Framework Programme for Research, Technological Development and Demonstration funded a demonstration project called iClass. That concept reduces the instructor's role in customized learning through a method called self-regulated personalized learning (SRPL). Self-regulation is where the learners, guided by an awareness of their learning style, choose activities and goals within the learning process. Other approaches include the use of computer software that adapts the presentation of content to the learner's style. Technological solutions such as these allow instructors to take on the role of a coach or mentor with expertise in the subject area but without the need for more highly developed teaching skills.

Software employing SRPL for specific Air Force skills may be prohibitively expensive and warrants a small-scale experiment to measure the actual return on investment (e.g., fewer instructors, faster graduation, etc.).

Given the extensive use of CBI in many current training contexts, it is clearly feasible to develop CBI modules for Air Force training contexts. This technology would facilitate the implementation of self-paced instruction, as discussed above. If CBI were used in a technical training environment, instructors would need to be present to answer questions, maintain oversight, demonstrate instruction, and provide safety. Where appropriate, students could break out of self-paced modules for fixed-time demonstrations or hands-on practice.

Customized Learning in the Air Force 2.0 Organization

The AETC white paper on the future of learning (2009) describes three concepts (knowledge management, continuous learning,[1] and precision learning) that form the basis for a new learning construct called *Air Force 2.0*:

> Successful operations in this and all warfighting domains require the adept leveraging of *knowledge management*, force development through *continuous learning*, and providing Airmen with the right skills and the knowledge to generate the right effect through *precision learning* delivery to prepare Airmen for the future. In the future environment, new Air Force learning capabilities management approaches will be required to capitalize on these concepts and leverage the new skills and abilities of knowledge-enabled Airmen. (p. 10, emphasis ours)

In this chapter, we look at customized learning as it applies to this new learning construct.

Knowledge Management

AETC (2009) defines *knowledge management* as

> the end-to-end continuous process that describes the systematic creation, acquisition, integration, distribution, application and archiving of knowledge to drive behavior and actions which support organizational objectives and mission accomplishment. (p. 11)

> A dynamic knowledge repository managed by subject matter experts and knowledge gatekeepers can ensure current and authoritative data is available whenever and wherever needed to support training, education and operations. (p. 11)

We see little potential for application of customized learning to knowledge management. However, the use of learning styles as a customized learning approach will increase the workloads involved in knowledge management, as it will demand additional efforts in the creation, acquisition, and integration of knowledge in alternate learning style forms. As more forms of knowledge emerge from knowledge management efforts, it becomes more likely that learners will find something that fits their style.

---

[1] While *continuous learning* is the term used in the Air Force 2.0 white paper, *lifelong learning* is the term most often seen in the literature and in the private sector.

Continuous Learning

AETC's white paper describes *continuous learning* as

> the ability to teach Airmen . . . to learn. Specifically, approaching Airman learning as a continuous and life-long process of training, education, and experiential learning that has as its outcome the development of Airmen who can individually recognize the right skills, knowledge, and aptitude they need to accomplish assigned tasks and missions. (p. 27)

Customized learning supports continuous learning because, as an individual better understands the way he or she learns, he or she can use that knowledge to pursue avenues of lifelong learning. Customized learning makes it easier for individuals to habituate to learning and find it congenial. It helps individuals realize why and where learning has been difficult in the past and what adjustments can make it more agreeable.

Precision Learning

AETC's white paper describes *precision learning* as

> delivering in a short, compressed period the appropriate education, training, or experience at the right time, in the right format, to generate the right learning effect. (p. 28)

Customized learning supports precision learning by maximizing the right learning effect at the right time and right place. Customized learning targets training to the learner, which is very much akin to tenets of precision learning, where learning is tailored to the needs of the individual. Inherent in this approach is blended learning, which utilizes multiple modes of instruction to deliver the right material to the learner.

Customized Learning Applied to Attributes of Air Force 2.0

Within the Air Force 2.0 learning construct are six attributes of a transformed education and training environment (Thompson, 2009). In this section, we discuss these attributes and their relationship to customized learning.

Learner-Centric Environment

Creating a learner-centric environment is a key feature of customized learning. It reduces emphasis on simply *transmitting* information to the student, instead seeking to ensure that the information is best processed by the learner. Too often in initial skills training, information is transmitted primarily through PowerPoint lectures, leaving the students to process the information as best they can. Later, tests measure how well the student processed the information. A poor performance forces the student to hurriedly attempt to reprocess the information before a quick retest. Failure on the second test leaves the organization with three choices:

1.   Send the student back to the beginning of the current block to again process the information.

2. Transfer the student to another career field to process simpler information.

3. Eliminate the student from the Air Force for failure to process.

Customized learning actively supports the learner-centric philosophy. The use of learning styles will challenge the new learning organization to create a range of alternative means of conveying information so that each student can process information most effectively.

Knowledge Bases

Customized learning will create new demands for greater use of knowledge bases. Customized learning requires information to be deliverable in different formats to accommodate the varied learning styles of users.

The expansion of knowledge bases in multiple formats (live, virtual, auditory, visual, problem-centered, etc.) would seem to be prohibitively expensive if pursued in the way in which current knowledge databases are built. Contractor-developed tools in proprietary formats and required contractor updates to maintain currency are likely to be too slow and too expensive. One solution is to harness the millennial generation's technological savvy to create the knowledge databases of the future.

Technical training course materials can be considered part of a knowledge base. In most Air Force schoolhouses, subject matter experts are split into two flights, one that does the teaching and one that develops the courseware knowledge base. However, the average instructor is increasingly technologically literate (by virtue of the job passing to the following generation), is able to develop courseware using increasingly user-friendly software for CBI, and would likely enjoy that part of the job. As CBI becomes more prevalent in technical training, the Air Force should consider selecting individuals with self-developed computer skills for assignment to training development roles.

Knowledge on Demand

If we extend the idea of customized learning from pace and style to time and place, then customized learning could increase the need for knowledge-on-demand systems. In the case of initial skills training, skills are developed to a limited level, to be supplemented by on-the-job training. With better and more available knowledge systems in the workplace, it will be possible to move additional portions of initial skills training into on-the-job training.

Cognitive/Affective Domains

Bloom's (1956) taxonomy lists three domains of educational activities: cognitive, affective, and psycho-motor. The Air Force has focused on the cognitive and psycho-motor domains in most training. The affective domain of feelings, values, motivations, and attitudes has less emphasis in the education process.[2] However, if the Air Force wants Airmen to internalize the values of the organization in order to be enthusiastic about its goals, more attention needs to be directed toward the affective domain.

In addition to the other benefits already highlighted, customized learning can increase the intrinsic motivation of the student to learn. As Aviram et al. (2008) observed,

---

[2] Special forces training and other elite training seem to emphasize the "attitude" more so than most jobs in the Air Force.

A fundamental premise of the self-regulated personalized learning framework is that by allowing growing levels of openness (choice), autonomy, self regulation, and personalisation of the learning process, so grows the students' intrinsic motivation. (p. 11)

Live, Virtual, Constructive Mix[3]

Today, online learning and virtual schools are providing individual access to learning opportunities—personalized not only to student learning needs and interests, but available when and where students are interested in learning, be that at home or at school. (U.S. Department of Education, 2008, p. 3)

The use of simulation can have a tremendous payoff for customized learning. Simulation provides an approach to learning that contrasts sharply with the sterile environment of a lecture. Virtual simulations provide users with a sense of the environment they will encounter in the Air Force. Simulations can challenge users with virtual problem solving and virtual games, thereby increasing the interest in the field of study. The power of live, virtual, constructive gaming is that it leverages learning through expectation and failure. This is particularly true of the integration of properly developed gaming applications.

Simulations are expensive to produce, but technological advances are changing the way simulations are created. Virtual simulations, such as the popular platform Second Life,[4] use simple tools that allow any user to create a broad variety of environments, with modest cost to the developer. The biggest problem the Air Force would have is not finding developers but rather maintaining control of all the virtual development.

We would not recommend the extensive use of Second Life on the open Internet for official Air Force training or developmental purposes. We think the concept has great value in a controlled environment, within the military intranet. Simulations can be transferred out of the intranet for limited public interaction and use as, for example, a recruiting tool. But the potential for unsavory material to be juxtaposed with or inserted into Air Force content in an open Second Life application suggests caution in using this approach.

Knowledge-Enabled Airmen

If a customized learning approach indeed creates individuals with the motivation and desire to be continuous learners, as some of the literature suggests (Coffield et al., 2004a, p. 119; Apter, 2001, p. 306), it likely can create knowledge-enabled Airmen. Already today, young Airmen know how to find knowledge through the Internet. Akande describes the rule of thumb for the technology-savvy generation as "don't ask until you've Googled" (2008, p. 20). Most apply this ability to social networks and personal interests. It is a small step to apply that to Air Force activities, especially among motivated learners. The tools of the millennial generation can transfer very easily into tools with military potential.

---

[3] The Army uses the term *live, virtual, constructive gaming.*

[4] Second Life is a virtual reality simulation in which individuals, called residents, create personal avatars and live virtually. Second Life applications include gaming, building, business, education, and social interaction, the primary activity in Second Life.

Customized Learning and the Instructor of the Future in Air Force 2.0

A number of the implications of customized learning are dependent on a new type of instructor. The Air Force will continue to draw subject matter experts from the field to teach courses in its schools—we do not recommend changes to this approach. Fortunately, the skills of that force will change over time. An AETC study (2008) on technology identified that younger Airmen are more technologically literate than older Airmen. As these younger Airmen become instructors, there is a great opportunity to take advantage of their technoliteracy.

Assuming that the Air Force pursues customized learning in some form, we offer the following as necessary shifts in instructor competencies:

- better able to put the learner first
- better able to understand learning styles for the benefit of helping the student develop as a learner
- better able to understand and apply pedagogical theory
- better able to be a lifelong learner (not just as an AFSC practitioner, but also as an educator)
- more technology-savvy, so that he or she can build simple computer-based training modules and interactive virtual worlds using open-source software.

CHAPTER FIVE

Leveraging Technology to Enhance Learning

We have seen our world change around us and now need to retool our education system to respond. Part of our challenge has been that technology has been applied to the outside of the education process, rather than as a critical tool in revamping the process itself. Personalizing instructional delivery through the strategic use of technology is a key part of that transformation. (U.S. Department of Education, 2008, p. 9)

Recent research has attempted to come to grips with the potential for new learning approaches and systems to transform learning. For example, Fairbanks (2009) is developing a learning operating model that addresses organizational structure, delivery modes, governance, and sourcing strategies. The model also includes content, information management and access (presence and effectiveness of design), development and management of content promoting standardization and reuse, and performance measurement (tools for monitoring and assessing learning efficiency and effectiveness). Similar technological tools are changing the face of education across the nation.

Chapman (2007) found that commercial-sector case studies have shown cycle time reduction and development savings from structural reuse within individual companies that employed learning content management systems to automate the development and delivery of content in multiple delivery formats (e.g., online courses, job aids, instructor guides, lesson plans, classroom visuals, tests, handouts) using a large central repository and one-time development of content.

The New Era of E-Learning and Learning Management Systems

Many terms have been used to describe e-learning. Web-based training, computer-based training, and online learning are a few examples. E-learning is simply a medium for delivering learning and covers a wide array of activities, from supported learning to blended or hybrid learning (the combination of traditional and e-learning practices) to learning that occurs 100 percent online. Sound e-learning is founded on instructional design principles and pedagogical elements that take learning theories into account ("About e-Learning," undated). Many companies and universities in the United States in recent years have taken advantage of e-learning, predominantly conducted over the Internet.

It is important to view e-learning as a tool and not as a panacea and to understand that for its employment to be effective, sound instruction design principles and pedagogical elements must still be taken into account. Thus, e-learning adapts to the individual by allowing him or her to set the learning pace according to his or her own optimal speed and, in some

As LMSs proliferated in colleges, and at a slower pace in businesses and local governments, both students and teachers began to compare advantages of the systems for potential customization of their own systems. Munoz and Van Duzer (2005) compared satisfaction levels of online teaching and learning tools. The experiment compared Moodle 1.3.2 with Blackboard 6.0 Basic Edition using a course previously taught in a classroom. The experimental approach was to teach one random assignment the first day of class, half in Blackboard, half in Moodle. The features of the two systems included

- electronic assignment submissions
- virtual areas for group work
- self-assessment quizzes and online testing
- sequential learning objects (Moodle only)
- embedded ShockWave Flash files
- tracked specific student activity (Moodle only)
- poll (Moodle only)
- glossary (Moodle only)
- survey
- discussion forums
- links to external web pages.

The polled facilitators responded that both Moodle and Blackboard had apparent competitive advantages. Moodle provided individualized feedback easily on all assignments. It also proved easier for the facilitator to track each student's activity in class—when, how often, and from where students access the course. Blackboard's advantages over Moodle were a more polished appearance, a better grade book, threaded discussions that easily differentiated between read and unread posts, and announcements that were more prominently displayed on entering the course.

Student satisfaction in this study was judged by a survey examining the following areas:

- Did Blackboard/Moodle enhance instruction?
- Did the user receive adequate technical assistance?
- Did the technology-based activities develop problem-solving skills?
- Were the instructional materials well organized?
- Were the web-based resources effective as learning tools?
- Were the discussion boards easy to use?
- Did this communication tool enhance interaction with instructors?
- Did this communication tool enhance interaction with classmates?

In the end, Munoz and Van Duzer's students favored Moodle over Blackboard by 35.7 percent to 21.4 percent, with a significant proportion showing no preference. Moodle's primary advantage was enhanced interactions with instructors and fellow classmates (Munoz and Van Duzer, 2005).

applications, to choose the types of exercises and reinforcing practice lessons that correspond to his or her inclinations and are thus most likely to hold his or her interest. But some people will still do better with a classic schoolroom setting, will benefit from more direction, and will require oversight. Rossett and Chan (2008), for example, report both good news and bad news about e-learning effectiveness. They relate that there are attributes that make e-learning programs more effective. The good news is that new technologies allow us to know who is learning, referring, and contributing—and who is not—and to make "blended" learning possible. Though e-learning has led to improvements in training and development, it does not automatically lead to a commensurate increase in participation and persistence. In fact, in some studies (Phillips and Burkett, 2007–2008), participants in e-learning programs were found to be less likely to follow through than in an instructor-led program. Nor does e-learning seem to alleviate dropout rates.

Rossett (2009) relates that in 2002, 15 percent of reporting organizations used technology for delivery of learning programs. By 2004, this jumped to 30 percent. She reports that the best organizations delivered 32 percent of all their learning content using technology. She also reports that 75 percent of tech-based learning was self-paced in 2002 and, more importantly, that 75 percent of all tech-based learning was online by 2004.

Rossett (2009) believes that examining the potential benefits of e-learning could help the Air Force more quickly assess the knowledge level of Airmen, prepare Airmen for today's irregular and counterinsurgency environments, and identify and deploy people who may have special talents and experience.

Combining Technologies into Learning Systems

Four companies currently dominate the learning systems market in the United States: Blackboard, Desire2Learn, Moodle, and Sakai.

Blackboard is learning management system (LMS) software partially owned by Microsoft that is funded by annual licensing fees. To date it has been adopted by major institutions, such as Ohio State University and the University of Cincinnati, and smaller ones, such as Humboldt State University. Other institutions, such as the Virginia Department of Education and Columbia College (Missouri), have adapted the Desire2Learn system (Desire2Learn, 2009).

Desire2Learn is an open-source software-extensible LMS. It is secure, scalable, and upgradeable (Desire2Learn, undated). Though it utilizes open-source software, it is not free and requires a license and maintenance contract. More than 80 four-year higher-education institutions are clients.

Moodle is open-source, free LMS software that is customizable by programming staff, flexible for the instructor and developer, and supported by programmers worldwide. It is considered by some to be an LMS and by others to be a virtual learning environment (Moodle, 2009). It is a free web application that educators can use to create effective online learning sites. Moodle has a large and diverse user community; there were more than 780,000 registered users just on the one Moodle site we visited, speaking more than 78 languages in 204 countries.

Sakai is distributed as free and open-source software under the Educational Community License ("Sakai: Product Overview," undated). Sakai refers to itself as a collaboration and learning environment. Sakai's open development process allows users to develop unique local applications. Sakai was founded in 2004 with a $2,200,000 initial grant from the Mellon Foundation and the Hewlett Foundation and with $4,400,000 from core partners. Some institutions, such as the Lancaster University Management School in the UK, run both Moodle- and Sakai-based courses for teaching and also for building communities of individuals (business professionals, participant research groups) and report that both have been successful (Zacker.org, 2009). In their view, success is more about ensuring that instructors are properly trained and resourced to make the switch than about the technology itself.

The experience of institutions such as the University of Cincinnati in integrating learning systems might have significant implications for ongoing Air Force customized learning efforts. The University of Cincinnati has been using a home-grown system, through trial and error for the last four years, to integrate different technologies, such as Turning Point's radio frequency–based "clicker" learning system[1] and the Blackboard learning system, in order to meet its own customized learning needs.

The Blackboard learning system offers the university, among other capabilities, an instant messaging system that allows real-time interaction between teachers and students. Currently 75 percent of courses taught at the university use the Blackboard system. University professors relate that the system enhances key teacher-student functions, such as automatic grading, checking for plagiarism, discussion boards, and a shared whiteboard. Though the University of Cincinnati has been using Blackboard for ten years, it has also integrated it with other learning systems, such as the Turning Point clicker system. The clicker system is being used for 50–60 larger courses at the University of Cincinnati and has been found to be teacher friendly because it integrates well with PowerPoint.

E-learning has not only grown by leaps and bounds in the United States over the last several years but also overseas. From January to March 2008, the Department of Computer Science at the University of Oviedo in Spain conducted a small survey on the use of web-based LMSs that is instructive (Figure 5.1).

Figure 5.1
University of Oviedo's Survey, "Web-Based LMS for Higher Education"

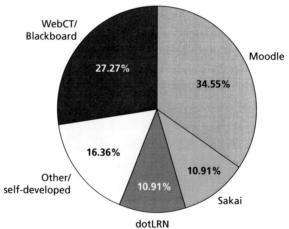

SOURCE: Department of Computer Science at the University of Oviedo, undated.
NOTE: Percentages represent the distribution of web-based learning systems among universities surveyed.
RAND *TR880-5.1*

---

[1] The "clicker" is a wireless keypad instrument given to (or purchased by) each student that gives immediate feedback to the instructor to questions asked. It integrates with PowerPoint presentations.

Technology and Learning Organizations

Holm (2009) relates that it is important for organizations to "sustain knowledge across missions and generations" and to "identify and capture the information that exists across the organization."[2] Also, a learning organization needs to help people find, organize, and share the knowledge they already have by efficiently managing the organization's knowledge resources. The most effective learning organizations increase collaboration and facilitate knowledge creation and sharing by developing techniques and tools that enable teams and communities to collaborate across barriers of time and space.

For the Air Force, Holm's observations might translate into questions like "How does the Air Force adopt information technology systems to capture some of the knowledge and skills of retiring employees?" Holm relates that "teaching" and "instructional modes of delivery" may be outmoded paradigm(s), and large organizations like the Air Force need to shift more resources toward sharing information *across* generations. To this end, her organization, NASA JPL, uses "Explorer Island" in Second Life not only for outreach, education, and training but also in an operational mode to support live missions, modeling and simulation, daily collaboration, and proposal development.

Mobile Versus Situated Learning Technologies

Brown, a member of the U.S. Army's Distributed Learning Subcommittee, believes that recent advances in what she terms "mobile learning" also have many implications for the Air Force (2009). In this context, mobility is no longer restricted to a matter of traveling but instead increasingly reflects the degree to which people can interact with information and others in new configurations of social-technical relationships *independent* of geographical proximity (Kakihara and Sorenson, 2002).

Brown's research starts with the proposition that "the teacher doesn't know everything." She relates that there is increasing discussion about advancing the "second screen" approach.[3] There is an increasing recognition by those who use new technologies that it is not only the teacher who imparts knowledge. In fact, new technologies enable the creation of new positions or third players—in addition to traditional teachers. Some universities are already making use of a "Google jockey" who contemporaneously searches the Web on behalf of the class as the discussion between student and teachers veers from topic to topic. Brown's research indicates a need to further examine dynamic ways to supplement the teacher in new learning environments. Teachers are already increasingly regarded as "facilitators" with the introduction of such systems and technologies.

---

[2]   Holm is the Chief Knowledge Architect at the Jet Propulsion Laboratory (JPL), California Institute of Technology. She leads the National Aeronautics and Space Administration's (NASA's) knowledge management team, and recent activities include transforming NASA into a learning organization through the use of communities of practice and sharing lessons learned.

[3]   The "second screen" is a handheld device supplementing instruction in the classroom (the first screen).

Opportunities for New Educational Technologies

The Air Force increasingly faces supporting core competencies and missions that present themselves as asymmetric challenges. Brown (2009) also suggested examining how new technologies could be used to close the gap between the interest (letter of intent) shown by potential recruits and their final commitment. It follows that the Air Force will need to tailor its teaching-learning approach and instructional modes of delivery to this new environment. Brown relates that Gottferdson's (2008) elements of learning may be instructive in this regard. His five elements are

- first-time learning
- additional learning
- trying to remember-recall
- learning during change
- learning when something goes wrong.

En masse, collaborative forms of social interaction have taken off in recent years among America's youth. In many ways, higher education has followed. The experience of Rush's High-Tech High School in San Diego, California, is instructive in this regard. The school was founded in 2000 and currently has an enrollment of 430 students, from grades 9 through 12 (Rush, 2009).

High-Tech High uses a unique learning approach focused less on competition and more on collaboration. It currently offers courses with titles such as

- 3-D Game Design
- Furniture from Junk
- First Robotics—Design and Build
- Independent Visual Arts Studio.

The High-Tech High experience has important implications for Air Force customized learning efforts. At High-Tech High, each student has a digital portfolio that can be accessed on the school's homepage. The portfolio construct offers important insights for attitudes and interests of new recruits as learners increasingly expect emphasis more on the teacher-guided "discovery" style of learning using Mosston and Ashworth's (1994) spectrum of teaching styles.[4]

Using Technology as a Resource, Not a Solution

For the Air Force, we draw three conclusions regarding the use of learning technology:

- Learning technologies hold the promise of mitigating some of the challenges its training programs confront by allowing greater responsiveness to the individual's learning style, prior knowledge, speed of learning, capabilities, and interests.

---

[4]   Mosston and Ashworth describe ten distinctive teaching styles based on the degree to which the teacher and/or students assume responsibility for what occurs in the lesson. Some aspects of customized learning assume greater responsibility of the student for the learning.

- A very large pool of applications from which to choose is available. These applications can be adapted, or entirely new ones can be developed.
- These applications are tools, not complete solutions.

Johnstone and Poulin commented that "it should be no surprise to learn that the most critical variables affecting the costs of using technology all relate to people" (2002, p. 21). In a university setting, they believe that the wrong person to develop technological solutions is the professor, given the relative salary levels of professors. In the Air Force, instructor salaries are equivalent to or less than most contracted courseware developers, and there may be savings associated with using government personnel to develop tools. These assumptions should also be tested in an experiment.

CHAPTER SIX

Recommendations

We recommend a series of experiments to test the effectiveness of customized learning and technological advances in education.

One experiment would focus on self-paced learning. The operations intelligence course would be a good candidate because it requires a large amount of memorization. The course also has a high attrition rate. Given that individuals memorize and retain information at different speeds, the experiment would examine the effect of allowing students to study the material at their own speeds. Simple video recordings could supplement a lack of current CBI, which may require buying headphones for listening.[1] Scripted PowerPoint lectures, reading material, and individual computers are already available for this course. An instructor would be required to monitor the class and provide personalized help as needed. Classes could start at any time, and larger class sizes could be utilized. Demonstrations or hands-on equipment would require fixed schedules so that students, having completed the prerequisites, could stop the self-paced work and attend, returning later to where they left off in the self-paced portion. Some safeguards would be required for testing (e.g., the use of multiple test questions to avoid cheating). Key criteria to examine would be the average length of time to graduation, average test scores, washback rates, attrition rates, required number of instructors to support, and overall costs. As a corollary to self-paced learning, an additional scenario would evaluate the advantages of eight-hour instructional days compared with the more common six-hour instructional day seen in the civilian world. The additional two hours have some self-pacing features in that they allow each student to use the time as he or she sees best.

We would also suggest a similar test in a high washback course, such as the Aerospace Ground Equipment course (AGE). This course would be significantly more difficult to use for experimentation because of the large amount of hands-on training and equipment use. It would require some creativity to create ongoing laboratories (equipment centers) with fixed or nonfixed starting times. Ultimately, using AGE for experimentation may be too difficult, but the concept of using self-pacing in a course with a high washback rate has merit.

We recommend administering a learning style instrument and providing a learning style assessment to students in a medium- or high-attrition course and evaluating the effects against classes without learning style feedback. We also suggest making some instructors aware of student learning styles and providing the instructors with some information on how to adapt their teaching styles to the students' learning styles. This experiment would have three experimental groups: (1) a control group with no learning style feedback, (2) students with learning style

---

[1]   If self-paced learning is successful, some savings could be devoted to better self-paced courseware than video recordings and existing scripted PowerPoint lectures.

feedback only, and (3) students with learning style information and instructors with information on how to adapt teaching styles.

We recommend administering a teaching style instrument and providing a teaching style assessment to instructors in a medium- or high-attrition course with a short two- to five-day workshop on how to use the results effectively. This should be supported by objective and subjective evaluations of the effects against classes without teaching style impact. This should use variations with classes using (1) no learning or teaching style instruments, (2) classes using both learning and teaching style instruments, and (3) classes using only learning style instruments.

We recommend the experimental use of some available learning technologies. Using Moodle or any other LMS, for example, one experiment might seek to determine how easy it is for non–computer skilled instructors to adapt and use the LMS in a teaching environment and what advantages and disadvantages they found in using the tool. A survey tool could be used pre- and post-experiment to assess ease of use, usefulness, required time to update, etc. Finally, some effort would be required to determine the overlap between the test LMS and the technical training management system.[2]

Similarly, another experiment would consider the use of Second Life for virtual problem solving. The same questions as before would be evaluated: usage by non–computer skilled instructors, advantages and disadvantages in using the tool, and student reaction to the virtual environment.

Some of the research was suggestive of a link between learning styles and occupation. If the Air Force measures learning styles, a corollary experiment would be to test learning styles against success in various occupations.

---

[2]   The technical training management system is an administrative tool with some similarities to an LMS for tracking student administrative details.

Bibliography

Abelson, Hal, and Phillip D. Long, "MIT's Strategy for Educational Technology Innovation, 1999–2003," in *Proceedings of the IEEE*, Vol. 96, No. 6, June 2008, pp. 1012–1034.

"About e-Learning," website, undated. As of September 30, 2009:
http://www.about-elearning.com

Air Education and Training Command (AETC), "On Learning: The Future of Air Force Education and Training," AETC White Paper, Randolph Air Force Base, Tex., January 30, 2008.

Air University, *Virtual World Learning . . . Simulation Gaming Kit for Education*, Air Force Document, November 26, 2008.

Aitoro, Jill R., "Cell Phones, Other Wireless Devices Next Big Cybersecurity Targets," *nextgov*, Nation Journal Group, Inc., June 17, 2009.

Akande, Benjamin Ola, "The I.P.O.D. Generation," *Diverse: Issues in Higher Education*, Vol. 25, No. 15, September 4, 2008, p. 20.

Al-Fahdi, Asma, and Kareema Al-Siyabi, "Mobile Learning," PowerPoint presentation on Slideshare.net, undated. As of September 30, 2009:
http://www.slideshare.net/tech4101/mobile-learning-presentation-805226

"APOSDLE Demo Storyboard," briefing on website, undated. As of September 30, 2010:
http://www.know-center.tugraz.at/forschung/knowledge_services/downloads_demos/
aposdle_demo_storyboard

Apter, M. J., *Motivational Styles in Everyday Life: A Guide to Reversal Theory*, Washington, D.C.: American Psychological Association, 2001.

Association of Personalized Learning Services, "Personalized Learning," 2009. As of November 6, 2009:
http://www.theaplus.org/personalized_learning.html

Aviram, Roni, "The Crisis of Modern Education in the Postmodern Era," *Navigating Through the Storm: Education in Postmodern Democratic Society*, draft English translation from Sense Publishers, original Hebrew published 1999, unpublished in English but available online, undated. As of September 30, 2009:
http://www.bgu.ac.il/futuredu/texts/Books.html

———, "Personalization and the iClass Project," Center for Futurism in Education, Ben-Gurion University, presentation at Eminent, Brussels, Belgium, December 6–7, 2007.

Aviram, Roni, Yael Ronen, Smadar Somekh, Yossi Schellas, Igal Dotan, and Amir Winer, *iClass Pedagogical Model and Guidelines*, report published by Information Systems Technologies under contract to the iClass Consortium, December 5, 2007.

Aviram, Roni, Ariel Sarid, Shiri Hagani, Yael Ronen, Amir Viner Roger Blamire, Paul Gerhard, Chris Jenkins, Eric Meyvis, and Christina Steiner, *The Future of Leaning? Results from the iClass Project*, Brussels, Belgium: European Schoolnet, June 2008.

Bamidis, Panagiotis D., Statis Th. Konstantinidis, Eleni Kaldoudi, Charalambos Bratsas, Maria M. Nikolaidou, Dimitris Koufogiannis, Nicos Maglaveras, and Costas Pappas, "New Approaches to Teaching Medical Informatics to Medical Students," in *IEEE Computer Society, 21st IEEE International Symposium on Computer-Based Medical Systems*, 2008, pp. 385–390.

Bloom, B. S., *Taxonomy of Educational Objectives, Handbook I: The Cognitive Domain*, New York: David McKay Co., Inc, 1956.

Brazell, Jim, and Danny Sharon, "Millennial Mind: Challenges of Changing Demographics in the Applicant Pool," PowerPoint briefing, Austin, Tex.: University of Texas, IC2 Institute, undated.

Brown, Judy, "Technology in Learning," interview with the authors, Middleton, Wisc., April 4, 2009.

Carey, Neil B., David L. Reese, David F. Lopez, Robert W. Shuford, and J. Katrine Wills, *Time to Train in Self-Paced Courses and the Return on Investment from Course Conversion*, Center for Naval Analysis (CNA), Alexandria, Va., March 2007.

Caruthers, Amy L., *Managing Generations: What the Air Force Can Learn from the Private Sector*, Maxwell Air Force Base, Ala.: Air Command and Staff College, April 2008.

Chapman, Bryan, "Reusability 2.0: The Key to Publishing Learning," white paper, Chapman Alliance, April 2007.

Clark, Richard, "K12 Speaker Series: Dr. Richard Clark on Mental Architecture and Consequences for Learning," notes from a lecture series, November 17, 2008.

Clarke, John, *Personalized Learning: Changing Systems to Personalize Learning*, The Education Alliance at Brown University, R.I., 2003.

Coffield, Frank, David Moseley, Elaine Hall, and Kathryn Ecclestone, *Learning Styles and Pedagogy in Post-16 Learning: A Systematic and Critic Review*, London: Learning and Skills Research Centre, 2004a.

———, *Should We Be Using Learning Styles?* London: Learning and Skills Research Centre, 2004b.

Cook, John, "Mobile Learning Group," PowerPoint presentation, London: Learning Technology Research Institute, London Metropolitan University, 2009. As of September 30, 2009:
http://www.slideshare.net/johnnigelcook/mobile-learning-group

Dawson, Kara, Cathy Cavanaugh, and Albert D. Ritzhaupt, "Florida's EETT Leveraging Laptops Initiative and Its Impact on Teaching Practices," *Journal of Research on Technology in Education*, Vol. 41, No. 2, Winter 2008–2009, pp. 143–159.

Dee, Lesley, Cristina Devecchi, Lani Florian, and Steve Cochrane, *Being, Having and Doing: Theories of Learning and Adults with Learning Difficulties*, London: Learning and Skills Research Centre, undated.

Department of Computer Science at the University of Oviedo, eLearning Survey, 2008. As of September 30, 2009:
http://www.di.uniovi.es/~victoralvarez/survey/

Desire2Learn, "Discover Desire2Learn—What Makes Us Unique?" undated. As of September 30, 2009:
http://www.desire2learn.com/discover/unique

———, "Resource Library," 2009. As of September 30, 2009:
http://www.desire2learn.com/resource/?a=02395jf82a

Diaz, David P., and Ryan B. Cartnal, "Students' Learning Styles in Two Classes: Online Distance Learning and Equivalent On-Campus," *College Teaching*, Vol. 47, No. 4, Fall 1999, pp. 130–135.

Docksai, Rick, "Teens and Cell Phones," *The Futurist*, January–February 2009, pp. 10–11.

Drysdale, M.T.B., J. L. Ross, and R. A. Schulz, "Cognitive Learning Styles and Academic Performance in 19 First-Year University Courses: Successful Students Versus Students at Risk," *Journal of Education for Students Placed at Risk*, Vol. 6, No. 3, 2001, pp. 271–289.

Duan Xinyu, Gu Baoqing, and Jiang Pin, "Concept and Application of Three Dimension Virtual Study Technology for Academic E-Learning," International Conference on Computer Science and Information Technology 2008, IEEE Computer Society, 2008, pp. 741–744.

E3: Employers for Education Excellence, Oregon Small Schools Initiative program, "Personalized Learning," 2005. As of November 6, 2009:
http://www.e3smallschools.org/pl.html

Ellis, Heidi J. C., "An Evaluation of Learning in an Online Project-Based Web Application Design and Development Course," *Consortium for Computing Sciences in Colleges: Northeastern Conference*, 2006, pp. 217–227.

Enriques, Amelito, Ananda Gunawardena, Frank Kowalski, Susan Kowalski, Don Millard, and Jim Vanides, "Innovations in Engineering Education Using Tablet PCs—Panel Discussion with Four Institutions," *36th ASEE/IEEE Frontiers in Education Conference*, October 28–31, 2006, Session S2B, pp. 1–2.

Fairbanks, Andrew, "Technology in Learning," interview with the authors, Washington, D.C., March 2, 2009.

Field, Sue, "Personalised Learning," *TTRB: Teacher Training Resource Bank*, October 6, 2006. As of September 30, 2009:
http://www.ttrb.ac.uk/viewArticle.aspx?contentId=12406

Foster, Paul, telephone interview with the authors, University of Cincinnati, Cincinnati, Ohio, April 2, 2009.

Galvin, Richard, "iClass, The European Schools: Experiences in Personalization," PowerPoint presentation, undated.

Gardley, Marlon K., Ryan F. Caulk, Leonardo Cardenas, and Peter Joffe, "Virtual Environment and Technology Survey at Keesler AFB Survey Report," Randolph Air Force Base, Tex.: AETC Studies and Analysis Squadron, August 29, 2009.

Gilbert, Christine, *2020 Vision: Report of the Teaching and Learning in 2020 Review Group*, Nottingham, UK: DfES Publications, December 2006.

Gill, Grandon, "Five (Really) Hard Things About Using the Internet in Higher Education," *eLearn Magazine*, Vol. 2006, No. 3, March 2006, p. 1.

Gottfredson, Conrad, "Learning at the Moment of Need," *Xyleme Voices: A Podcast Library on the Evolution of Training*, 2008.

Govindarajan, Vijay, and Chris Trimble, "Strategic Innovation and the Science of Learning," *MIT Sloan Management Review*, Winter 2004, pp. 67–75.

Hargreaves, David, Jackie Beere, Maggie Swindells, Derek Wise, Charles Desforges, Usha Goswami, David Wood, Matthew Horne, and Hannah Lownsbrough, *About Learning*, Report of the Learning Working Group, Demos, London, June 2004.

Hattie, John, "Influences on Student Learning," speech delivered at Inaugural Lecture: Professor of Education, University of Auckland, August 2, 1999.

Hattie, John, John Biggs, and Nola Purdie, "Effects of Learning Skills Interventions on Student Learning: A Meta-Analysis," *Review of Educational Research*, Vol. 66, No. 2, Summer 1996, pp. 99–136.

Hattie, John, and H. W. Marsh, "The Relationship Between Research and Teaching: A Meta-Analysis," *Review of Educational Research*, Vol. 66, No. 4, Winter 1996, pp. 507–542.

Hawk, Thomas F., and Amit J. Shaw, "Using Learning Style Instruments to Enhance Student Learning," *Decision Sciences Journal of Innovative Education*, Vol. 5, No. 1, January 2007, pp. 1–19.

Headquarters Second Air Force, 2AF/DOTF, "Plan of Instruction (Technical Training): Basic Instructor Course," Keesler Air Force Base, Miss., August 1, 2008.

Holm, Jeanne, telephone interview with the authors, Pasadena, Calif.: NASA JPL, March 1, 2009.

Hrastinski, Stefan, "Asynchronous and Synchronous E-Learning," *EDUCAUSE Quarterly*, Vol. 31, No. 4, October–December 2008.

ICT Results, "Personalized Learning Puts Students in a Class of Their Own," *ScienceDaily*, November 4, 2008. As of September 30, 2009:
http://www.sciencedaily.com/releases/2008/10/081027144645.htm

Johnstone, Sally M., and Russell Poulin, "So, How Much Do Educational Technologies Really Cost?" *Change*, March/April 2002, pp. 21–23.

Jones, Cheryl, Carla Reichard, and Kouider Mokhtari, "Are Students' Learning Styles Discipline Specific?" *Community College Journal of Research and Practice*, Vol. 27, No. 5, June 1, 2003, pp. 363–375.

Junglas, Iris A., Norman A. Johnson, Douglas J. Steele, D. Chon Abraham, and Paul Mac Loughlin, "Identity Formation, Learning Styles and Trust in Virtual Worlds," *The DATA BASE for Advances in Information Systems*, Vol. 38, No. 4, November 2007, pp. 90–96.

Kakihara, Masao, and Carsten Sorensen, "'Post-Modern' Professional Work and Mobile Technology," in *Proceedings of the 25th Information Systems Research Seminar in Scandinavia*, Bautahoj, Denmark, August 10–13, 2002.

Kaldis, Emmanouil, Konstantinos Koukoravas, and Christos Tjortjis, "Reengineering Academic Teams Toward a Network Organizational Structure," *Decision Sciences Journal of Innovative Education*, Vol. 5, No. 2, July 2007, pp. 245–266.

Kiyan, Carlos, et al., "mLearning for Health Care Workers in Low Resource Settings," PowerPoint presentation by the Institute of Tropical Medicine, Antwerp, and the Institute of Tropical Medicine, Alexander Von Humboldt, Lima, 2008.

Knuteson, Scott, "MyBase Offers Air Force Perspective in Virtual World," Air University Public Affairs, December 3, 2008. As of December 29, 2008:
http://www.aetc.af.mil/news/story.asp?id=123126415

Kostovich, Carol T., Michele Poradzisz, Karen Wood, and Karen L. O'Brien, "Learning Style Preference and Student Aptitude for Concept Maps," *Journal of Nursing Education*, Vol. 46, No. 5, May 2007, pp. 225–231.

Krasner, Steve, ed., *Learning Styles*, Connecticut State Department of Education, SERC Library, 2002. As of September 30, 2009:
http://www.ctserc.org/library/bibfiles/learning-styles.pdf

Laurillard, Diana, "Modelling Benefits-Oriented Costs for Technology Enhanced Learning," *Higher Education*, No. 54, 2007, pp. 21–39.

Lichtenstein, Olivia, "How the Faceless and Amoral World of Cyberspace Has Created a Deeply Disturbing Generation SEX," MailOnline, January 28, 2009. As of September 30, 2009:
http://www.dailymail.co.uk/femail/article-1129978/How-faceless-amoral-world-cyberspace-created-deeply-disturbing--generation-SEX.html

Linden Lab, *Virtual World Simulation Training Prepares Real Guards on the US–Canadian Border: Loyalist College in Second Life*, Linden Lab Case Study, San Francisco, Calif., 2009. As of November 6, 2009:
http://secondlifegrid.net.s3.amazonaws.com/docs/Second_Life_Case_Loyalist_EN.pdf

Lindsey, Jill, *21st Century Training for 21st Century Learners: A Pilot Research Study*, Dayton, Ohio: Wright State University, January 2009a.

———, "Anticipating Job-Aiding Requirements: 21st Century Training for 21st Century Learners," briefing presented to RAND researchers, February 22, 2009b.

Lovelace, Maryann Kiely, "Meta-Analysis of Experimental Research Based on the Dunn and Dunn Model," *The Journal of Educational Research*, Vol. 98, No. 3, January/February 2005, pp. 176–183.

Ludwig, Barbara, and B. J. Schone, "Virtually Anywhere: A Case Study of Mobile Learning at Qualcomm," PowerPoint briefing from Qualcomm, undated.

Martinez, Margaret, "What Is Personalized Learning?" *The eLearning Developers' Journal*, May 7, 2002a, pp. 1–8.

———, "Adaptive and Personalized Learning: Supporting Individual Learning Differences," Successful Learning Research Team, June 2002b. As of September 30, 2009:
http://www.trainingplace.com/source/research/masspersonalization.htm

Mayrath, M. C., and S. M. B. O'Hare, *A Proposed Method for Converting Squadron Officer School into a Blended-Learning Course with Live, Virtual, and Constructive Simulations*, University of Texas, Austin, Institute for Advanced Technology, February 2009.

McClelland, Bob, "Digital Teaching, Learning and Program Supports: An Examination of Developments for Students in Higher Education," *IEEE*, 1089-6503/00, 2000, pp. 43–49.

————, "Digital Learning and Teaching: Evaluation of Developments for Students in Higher Education," *European Journal of Engineering Education*, Vol. 26, No. 2, June 2001, pp. 107–115. As of November 6, 2009: http://www.informaworld.com/smpp/content~db=all~content=a713664526~frm=titlelink

McClintock, Robbie, *Power and Pedagogy: Transforming Education Through Information Technology*, New York: Institute for Learning Technologies, 1992.

McClintock, Robbie, and Frank Moretti, *The Cumulative Curriculum: Multi-Media and the Making of a New Educational System: A Project Description*, New York: Institute for Learning Technologies, 1991.

Moodle, home page, 2009. As of September 2009: http://moodle.org/

Mosston, M., and S. Ashworth, *Teaching Physical Education (4th ed.)*, Columbus, Ohio: Merrill Publishing Company, 1994.

Moura, Adelina, "Mobile Generation: Learning Environment Support on Mobile Technologies," PowerPoint presentation on Slideshare.net, 2008. As of September 30, 2009: http://www.slideshare.net/linade/mobile-learning-330315

Munoz, Kathy D., and Joan Van Duzer, "Blackboard vs. Moodle: A Comparison of Satisfaction with Online Teaching and Learning Tools," February 15, 2005. As of September 30, 2010: http://users.humboldt.edu/joan/moodle/all.htm

National Academy of Engineering of the National Academies, "Grand Challenges for Engineering: Advance Personalized Learning," undated, Washington, D.C. As of November 6, 2009: http://www.engineeringchallenges.org/cms/8996/9127.aspx

Nickson, Christopher, "The History of Social Networking," Digital Trends, January 21, 2009. As of September 30, 2009: http://news.digitaltrends.com/feature/99/the-history-of-social-networking-printer-friendly

Oslington, Paul, "The Impact of Uncertainty and Irreversibility on Investments in Online Learning," *Distance Education*, Vol. 25, No. 2, October 2004, pp. 233–242.

Pearson, "Personalized Learning: The Nexus of 21st Century Learning and Educational Technologies," *Pearson Issue Papers*, No. 3, July 21, 2009. As of November 6, 2009: http://www.pearsoned.com/pr_2009/072109.htm

The Personalized Learning Foundation, Inc., "What Is Personalized Learning?" undated. As of November 6, 2009: http://www.personalizedlearningfoundation.org/id3.html

Petrenko, Anatoly, "The Research and Development of the Modern Educational Technologies for Information Society," *TCSET 2004*, Lviv-Slavsko, Ukraine, February 24–28, 2004, pp. 2–4.

Phillips, Jack, and Holly Burkett, "The Business Value of E-Learning," *Elearning!* December 2007/January 2008, pp. 33–35.

Prashnig, Barbara, "10 False Beliefs About Learning Cause High Stress and Burnout in Teachers," *Education Today*, June 1994.

————, "Help, My Teacher Doesn't Know My Learning Style!" *Education Today*, No. 3, Term 2, 2000a, pp. 13–14.

————, "Learning Styles—Here to Stay," *Education Today*, No. 2, Term 2, 2000b, pp. 30–31.

————, "Learning Style Analysis: Pyramid Model," web page, Prashnig Style Solutions, undated. As of September 20, 2009: http://www.creativelearningcentre.com/Products/Learning-Style-Analysis/Pyramid-Model.html

The Principals' Partnership, a Program of Union Pacific Foundation, "Personalized Learning in the High School," research brief summarizing findings, undated. As of November 6, 2009: http://www.principalspartnership.com/personalizedlearning.pdf

Rayner, Stephen, and Richard Riding, "Towards a Categorisation of Cognitive Styles and Learning Styles," *Educational Psychology*, Vol. 17, Nos. 1 and 2, 1997, pp. 5–27.

Reynolds, P. F., Jr., C. Milner, and T. Highley, "Scalable Personalized Learning," *Frontiers in Education, 2004*, October 20–23, 2004, pp. 3–8.

Riesbeck, Christopher K., Lin Qui, Baba Kofi Weusijana, Joseph T. Walsh, and Matthew Parsek, "Learning Technologies to Foster Critical Reasoning: Focusing on Challenge-Based Learning Activities That Are Effective for Long-Term Learning," *IEEE Engineering in Medicine and Biology Magazine*, July/August 2003, pp. 55–57, 117.

Rossett, Allison, telephone communication with the authors, San Diego State University, San Diego, Calif., March 13, 2009.

Rossett, Allison, and Antonia Chan, *Engaging with the New eLearning*, white paper, San Jose, Calif.: Adobe Systems Incorporated, 2008.

Rossett, Allison, and Gerald Marino, "If Coaching Is Good, Then E-Coaching Is . . . ," *American Society for Training and Development*, November 2005, pp. 46–49.

Rush, Simi, "Technology in Learning," interview with the authors, San Diego, Calif., March 20, 2009.

"Sakai: Product Overview," website, undated. As of September 30, 2009:
http://sakaiproject.org/product-overview

Sandman, Thomas, "Gaining Insight into Business Telecommunications Students Through the Assessment of Learning Styles," *Decision Sciences Journal of Innovative Education*, Vol. 7, No. 1, January 2009, pp. 295–320.

Savill-Smith, Carol, Jill Attewell, and Geoff Stead Tribal, *Mobile Learning in Practice: Piloting a Mobile Learning Teacher's Toolkit in Further Education Colleges*, London: Learning and Skills Network, 2006.

Schmees, Markus, "Organizing Technology Enhanced Learning," in *Proceedings of the Eighth International Conference on Electronic Commerce (ICEC '06)*, Fredericton, New Brunswick, Canada, August 14–16, 2006, pp. 139–150.

Sebba, Judy, Nick Brown, Susan Steward, Maurice Galton, Mary James, Nicola Celentano, and Peter Boddy, *An Investigation of Personalized Learning Approaches Used by Schools*, University of Sussex, UK, 2007.

Shanley, Michael G., Matthew W. Lewis, Susan G. Straus, Jeff Rothenberg, and Lindsay Daugherty, *The Prospects for Increasing the Reuse of Digital Training Content*, Santa Monica, Calif.: RAND Corporation, MG-732-OSD, 2009. As of September 20, 2010:
http://www.rand.org/pubs/monographs/MG732/

Shim, J. P., and Chengqi Guo, "Weblog Technology for Instruction, Learning, and Information Delivery," *Decision Sciences Journal of Innovative Education*, Vol. 7, No. 1, January 2009, pp. 171–193.

Sikes, Carol S., Adelaide K. Cherry, William E. Durall, Michael R. Hargrove, and Kenneth R. Tingman, *Brilliant Warrior: Information Technology Integration in Education and Training*, a research paper presented to Air Force 2025, Maxwell Air Force Base, Ala., April 1996.

Sitzmann, Traci, "Improving Learning from Web-Based Training Courses: Research Evidence," PowerPoint briefing, Alexandria, Va.: Advanced Distributed Learning Co-Laboratory, October 2007.

Sitzmann, Traci, Katherine Ely, and Robert Wisher, "Designing Web-Based Training Courses to Maximize Learning," *Computer-Supported Collaborative Learning: Best Practices and Principles for Instructors*, Hershey, Pa.: IGI Global, 2008.

Sitzmann, Traci, Kurt Kraiger, David Stewart, and Robert Wisher, "The Comparative Effectiveness of Web-Based and Classroom Instruction: A Meta-Analysis," *Personnel Psychology*, Vol. 59, 2006, pp. 623–664.

Space for Personalised Learning, "Personalised Learning: A Policy Overview," London, 2007. As of September 30, 2009:
http://www.space4pl.org/resources/uploads/Personalised_Learning_Policy_Overview_100409_web.pdf

Stricker, Andrew, "Toward New Horizons: The Birth of Huffman Prairie in Cyberspace," research paper, Future in Air Force Education, undated. As of August 24, 2010:
http://future.af.edu/Future%20Library/Huffman-Prairie-Stricker2.doc

Stricker, Andrew G., and Larry Clemons, "Simulation Gaming for Education in MyBase: The Future of Air Force Education and Training with Virtual World Learning," undated. As of September 30, 2009: http://www.au.af.mil/au/aunews/archive/2009/0408/Articles/StrickerMMSPaper.pdf

Teoh, Belinda S. P., and Tse-Kian Neo, "Innovative Teaching: Using Multimedia to Engage Students in Interactive Learning in Higher Education," *IEEE Xplore*, April 1, 2006.

Thompson John, "On Learning: The Future of Air Force Education and Training," briefing, Randolph Air Force Base, Tex.: Air Education and Training Command, February 18, 2009.

Torrance, Harry, Helen Colley, Dean Garratt, Janis Jarvis, Heather Piper, Kathryn Ecclestone, and David James, *The Impact of Different Modes of Assessment on Achievement and Progress in the Learning and Skills Sector*, London: The Learning and Skills Research Centre, 2005.

TRADOC Distributed Learning Directorate, *Distributed Learning Enterprise Summit Review Report*, proceedings from summit held December 8–12, 2008, Old Dominion, Va., May 2009.

Turker, Ali, Ilhami Gorgun, and Owen Conlan, "The Challenge of Content Creation to Facilitate Personalized eLearning Experiences," paper in support of iClass project, Siemens Business Services eLearning Group, Ankara, Turkey, and Department of Computer Science, Trinity College, Dublin, Ireland, undated.

Turker, M. A., Ilhami Gorgun, and Owen Conlan, "The Challenge of Content Creation to Facilitate Personalized eLearning Experiences," *International Journal on E-Learning (IJEL)*, Vol. 5, January 2006.

U.S. Department of Education, *Harnessing Innovation to Support Student Success: Using Technology to Personalize Education*, Washington, D.C., 2008.

Webber, Sheila, "Second Life for Business: Ten Techniques," *FUMSI*, October 2008. As of September 30, 2009:
http://web.fumsi.com/go/article/use/3326

Webber, Sheila, and Sheila Yoshikawa, "Collaborating in Second Life," PowerPoint presentation from European Business School Librarians Group Conference, May 2009.

Xiaoquing Li, "Intelligent Agent-Supported Online Education," *Decision Sciences Journal of Innovative Education*, Vol. 5, No. 2, July 2007.

Zacker.org blog, "Sakai vs. Moodle," October 13, 2009. As of August 24, 2010:
http://www.zacker.org/sakai-project-vs-moodle